Acknowledgement

Above all, I want to give thanks to God for allowing me to grow through the struggles because without the struggles this book would not have existed. I want to thank my husband, Darell Garnett and my children, along with the rest of my family, each who supported and encouraged me to finish my goal by writing this book. I have many dear friends to thank and some of you I have found along the journey of writing this book, and others that have been by my side. I want to express my gratitude to the key people who help me give life to this book: Lorenzo Jones, Holleonna Mack, Alicia Benson, Alonna Harrison, Mery Burgener, Karen Madlock, John Chatmon, and Pastor David Roberson. They have encouraged me through the rough spots, read my draft, offered valid commentary, edited, proofread and designed my book cover.

Last but not least, I beg forgiveness to all those who supported me over this past year and whose name I failed to mention. Many have contributed to the production of this book in one way or another and I want to thank you.

- Content

- Acknowledgment

- Introduction

Introduction

Have you ever found yourself wanting to be free from so much heavy baggage from your past? Are you tired of your past getting in your way? Have you ever just wanted to lay it all down, and leave it all there for once and for all? To do so means sharing what you been through, with yourself and with others and facing things we hate most, judgment!

In this book, I will share things that most people would rather take to their grave. I will show you how embracing your truth and sharing it will not only free you, but will also help others break away from bondage and begin living a life full of hope and purpose. I am where I am today, because I finally got tired of allowing my past to hurt my present, and interrupt my future that God has for me. I came to understand that it was time to shed the guilt and shame and be restored so I could walk forward with my head held high into my purpose. I was being called by God but I was slow to answer because of shame and guilt. By God's Grace and Mercy, I was renewed. I knew then that I wanted to put my story on paper to let others know they are not alone.

We have all been through some things, by the time you're done reading this book, you will probably have gone through something else. So never forget there is hope, hope to trust in, to wait for, to look for or to desire something or someone. Hope is a feeling of expectation or desire for certain things to happen. We all have made mistakes, and we all have some good and bad things happen to us, but we seem to hold on to the bad and forget about all the good things.

I wonder how many others have struggled or have been struggling with this same issue. I asked God, how could I be an inspiration to help someone? I feel as if God answer was for me share my lesson to keep others from delaying their blessing. I want others to know in your darkest time that there is still light and that is with God, it is not over for you or me.

Throughout this book, I am transparent about the struggles and the issues I have faced. I am brutally honest about myself I am not worried about judgment, for no one could ever judge me as harshly as I judge myself for all those years. You will also travel with me on the journey of healing, and learn where I found hope, and also you will learn that I am still picking up pieces.

Chapter 1:

This Is Where It All Started

I was born and raised in a low- income apartment called Wayne Minor Court Housing on 12th Street in Kansas City, Missouri. Wayne Minor Projects was built in 1962 for military families and then it transitions into low-income families that were in poverty. The "projects" had six high rise buildings that were located down north. My grandmother moved to Wayne Minor Projects 1965, were she raised eleven of her children, some of her children left as they got older, and others stayed. My mom was one of the ones that stayed in the projects. My family and I lived on the fourth floor in the 2011 building. This place had a reputation for drugs, prostitution, bad living conditions and violence.

My mother started having children at the age of nineteen and had me and my twin sister at the age twenty- four. She was a young mother raising five kids, some days we had a babysitter so my mother can get out and hang out with her friends. My mother was a product of her environment, and she was comfortable with her situation because that all she has seen.

On one Saturday evening, my sisters and I were playing around the house. My oldest sister, which was five years old at the time, helped my mother out with us a lot. My mother told her to put me and my twin sister in the bathtub. I don't recall where my mother went after that. We got in the tub and I was the closest one to the faucets. My five-year-old oldest sister mistakenly turned on the hot water. I was injured with second-degree burns on my right hand, legs, and feet. I screamed and cried so loud because it hurt so badly. (If you ever lived in the projects you know that the hot water really gets hot.) My skin turned red and bubbly and it felt so horrible. I didn't know what to do but stand there and just scream and cry. My twin sister jumped out of the bathtub screaming and was so scared because she saw that I was hurt. My oldest sister ran as fast as she could to go find my mother, which I still don't recall where she was. We were all so young at that time; the oldest boys were nine and four, and the girls were five and three years of age. My mother was in her twenties raising five kids. (Can you imagine?) My mother came running and saw what had happened and she immediately got scared and started to panic and cry, she didn't know what to do. She picked me up, put me on the bed and covered me up. I was just lying there, crying in pain, my mother was so scared she was pacing back and forth, back and forth.

She knew I needed to go to the hospital, but she also knew what they would do to her and to me. I was in the bed in pain unable to walk, trying to figure out what did I do to deserve this, pleading and crying can somebody please help me!

Finally, two hours later she took me to the doctor and just as she knew, it happened. My mother was charged with child abuse and neglect.

Division Family Service (DFS) got involved and I did not return home. They kept me at the hospital for two weeks and they did major surgery. They ended up taking skin from my bottom area and put it on my hand. I was crying for my mother and wanted to go home, but I did not. I did not return home until about two years later. Division of Family Service put me in foster care; I was sad and scared and didn't understand. I remember thinking "Why doesn't she want me?"

My foster mom, as I can remember had a very nice home and was nice to me. She made sure I had everything I need and wanted, but it just didn't feel like my home, where my family was. My foster mom took me back and forth to visit my family, and I felt that my brothers and sisters didn't know me anymore. My twin sister and I were very close, but she would just sit there and stare at me and cry. It made me feel really sad.

Two years later, I returned home with my birth mother, I had to get to know my siblings all over again, and I enjoyed every minute of it. I was so happy to be back at home, we all grew up together in a three bedroom room apartment that wasn't the best.

Our apartment had so many roaches that we couldn't turn off the light in our kitchen, that's how bad it was. We were not the only ones living like this; the whole building was infested with bugs and mice. There were plenty of times we were left home with my older brother and didn't have anything to eat. There were days we had milk and no cereal if we had cereal, there was no milk. We would eat sugar bread and drink sugar water. We even had to eat hard noodles, because we were told to stay away from the stove. The only time we had everything we needed, was the first of the month for about three weeks. When we ran out of food, we had to go to the food pantry and the soup kitchen to eat and get a box of food. My mother had to make the food last until she got her food stamps. We were raised on powdered milk, government cheese, beans and food stamps. Even though time was very hard, we struggled together and made it through.

We had to experience not having electricity or gas. My mother had to make a decision on which bills she can pay that month, she was on welfare and it wasn't much. We had to light candles to see, or we had to warm water to take a bath. We also had to wash our clothes out in the tub on a scrub board with no soap powder.

My great-grandmother came over to take my older brother to church with her, and then he started spending the night and finally he moved in with her. I knew it was a big relief for my mother, but also I know she wished he was there to help her with us.

As we got older, we notice that this man was coming around a lot and eventually he moved in. He was not a really nice man he was very abusive to my mother. She was very quiet and soft-spoken and he took advantage of her, unfortunately, there was nothing I could do about it. My mother's boyfriend used to bring his family around and they would sit around, get drunk, curse and talk loudly. Some of his family members just moved into her home, and my mother wouldn't say anything. I was wishing that maybe one day my mother would speak up. When he got drunk, he would start mistreating her, some days we liked him, but most of the time we didn't. We were all young and didn't know any better, but we knew it was not right. We couldn't say anything because we knew we would get a whooping from him.

This was an every weekend occurrence he would get drunk, act a fool, and make us dance around the table to the blues music (BB King). We thought it was fun, so we did it, but eventually in his drunkenness, he would try to fight my mother. Most of the times one of my uncles had to come and help my mother, I was always happy when he did. I felt sorry for my mother and wish she would just leave him alone, but she kept letting him back in, and the abuse continued on for a lot more years.

"Remember, stop asking why they keep doing it and start asking why you keep allowing it." Author unknown

Chapter 2:

The Struggles In School

During elementary school, I remember getting picked on because my hair was short, and I didn't have the best-looking clothes. Some of the boys used to say, "A is for apple, J is for jack Carmen don't got no hair in the back." This went on every day, all through elementary school, so I put up a wall, ready to fight whoever had something negative to say about me. My mother couldn't afford to get me new clothes for school. However, I told myself that I wasn't going to let anybody get away with intimidating me Instead, I became

the bully.

When I began middle school, I continue

to cover up my pain by acting up in school.

The things I have seen my mother go through

had a big effect on me during my school years.

She was not only in an abusive relationship she

also was struggling to raise us.

Majority of the time I didn't eat

breakfast, and the most I ate was during lunch

at school. I didn't know if I would eat dinner

that night or not. Through all the stuff that was

going on at home, I was not a happy child I act out all through school.

My mother had to come pick me up from school at least once a week because I getting into so many fights. I was picking on girls who looked and dressed better than me. I really acted up in middle school; I don't even know how I made it out of that school, on to the ninth grade. All I was doing was taking my anger and frustration out on others, based on the way I was feeling and living.

I got expelled from the middle school for continuing to act out. I was having so many fights that didn't have anything to do with me.

I just wanted to be known and wanted other students to be scared of me, so I could feel like I had some control. I couldn't go to my high school in the area I was living in because I got kicked out of the district. I had to go enroll in a school in another area. The high school that I attended in ninth grade was a nightmare for me, the girls there did not play, I started to get picked on and I got scared. (What goes around comes around), so I decided to drop out of school. I didn't want to get picked on and I couldn't be the bully anymore. At this point, I felt like there was no hope for me and I wasn't focused at all. I was struggling with all my classes, the school was getting harder for me, I hadn't paid attention in middle school, and

everything was closing in on me. I decided to

drop out, didn't have any plans, no money, no

job or anything. I can't recall my mother

saying anything about my dropping out of

school, she really didn't say much.

After being out of school for some years I

decided to go enroll in a GED program. I

enrolled in a General Education Program

(GED) at the Kansas City library. I started off

really good, going every day, and doing my

work. Then I fell off, got distracted and stop

going. I knew I wanted to get it together, but I was distracted and I needed someone to hold my hand and I just didn't have that. I was just left out there to figure it out on my own. Every program I enrolled in, I didn't complete. I wanted my friends to sign up with me, and if they didn't go, I wasn't going either. I felt like I had to have friends around, in order for me to do something positive.

Chapter 3

Young and lost

Not long after I dropped out school, I move out of my mother's house and moved in with one of my friends. I thought I had it all together because I had a nice shape and a pretty smile. I became buck wild, started hanging out, drinking, partying and doing what I wanted to do. I wasn't staying at my mother house anymore, so I figured that this is the way my life was going to be. I didn't know any other way. I was a fifteen-years-old, high school dropout and thought I really had it all together. I was getting up every day doing the same thing, kicking it and hanging out. I sought attention from any boy that came around, it didn't matter who they were or how they looked I just wanted the attention. I started hanging out in Kansas City, Kansas and other low- income projects. It was told to me that it was a lot of guys in these areas, so that is what my friend and I started doing.

I met plenty of boys, but one guy stood out to me, I knew he was in a gang. I didn't care because that is all I was attracted to. He did all kinds of wrong things and I was turned on. I was so attracted to the street boys, and starting seeing him, thinking I could get him to fall in love with me by dropping my pants. Going to different parties meeting him there, he gave me what I thought was love, he made me feel like a woman. I enjoy spending time with him when he was around. He spent more time in the street than at home, some days I would catch the bus to go look for him, I would go back to his mom's house and cry myself to sleep.

We were together for about six months and I got pregnant. I thought I was in love, I moved in with him and his mother. He was so excited about the baby and he decided that he wanted to turn his life around. He signed up for the Air Force he felt that the Air Force was his way out, from the streets. Unfortunately, he didn't make it, he was shot and killed when I was seven months pregnant. I felt like my whole life was ending, my boyfriend, the father of my baby was gone. It seems like everything just kept happening to me, no matter how hard I tried.

As I was faced with bringing my son into this world by myself, things seem to get worse. My doctor, that was caring for me and my unborn son at the time, stated that my baby had too much fluid around his head. It was a possibility that he could be born with Cerebral Palsy. I didn't know what to do or think, here I am expecting a baby they might have some issues. I didn't have a job; I dropped out of school, I'm living with his mom, the baby father is no longer here, I was devastated and young. We talked about marriage, having more children, getting our life together. The dreams we both had, all went away. I was lost and had no one to turn to, I couldn't believe that this sixteen-year old lost girl, have to experience this tragedy. What could be next, I was heartbroken, speechless, and confused, it didn't seem real but it was.

After all that was going on I knew I had to face reality. Two months later I gave birth to a healthy little boy, I named him after his father. Lying in the hospital bed holding my son crying, because I was all alone and he didn't have a father. It was really hard for me to accept it but I had to. I had a lot of support from my friends, but not what I needed, my son needs a father and he was no longer with us. Having my son at a young age, I went back to what I use to do, seeking attention, sleeping around, and having what I called was fun.

When my son turned six months I enrolled in Job Corps, trying to get my GED

32

and take up a trade. Job Corp gave my baby free daycare and they took me and some of the other girls to sign up for section 8 housing. Two months later, I got my section eight voucher and moved into my first two bedroom apartment.

In Job Corps, we study for our Ged and we had an opportunity to take up a trade. I got evaluated every two to three months, I didn't have my points in a timely manner and I immediately got kicked out. I was unfocused still no Ged.

My son was eight months at the time. I was enjoying my own space. Being on section 8, my rent was twenty-three dollars and yes twenty-three dollars! Truth be told, half of the time, I couldn't even pay that. It was sad, I had so many people running in and out of my house; my house was the hangout. You would think that all these people running in and out of my house, they can at least help me pay twenty-three dollars rent. At that time, I was blind to all that and didn't take my living hood serious.

The landlord was threatening to put me out because I couldn't pay my rent, and I had people running in and out, however, he felt sorry for me and let me stay. It was hard, and I just can't seem to get it right.

Chapter 4

Promiscuous Ways

Having my own place I felt like I was grown, I can do what I want. I was an attention seeker, so anyone who showed me some kind of interest, I would have sex with them. I felt like that's what I needed and wanted. I was looking for love through men.

Two years, of sleeping around I got pregnant with my second child, which was a girl. I named her after who I thought was her father at that time. Three years later we took a DNA test and the test came back, stating that YOU ARE NOT THE FATHER! I was convincing myself that test cannot be true he was the only one I was sleeping with. I was lying to him and to myself so he can still be with me. I was really sleeping around, and I wasn't for sure who her father was.

During my pregnancy, my oldest son father's best friend got released from prison and began helping me out with my son. He was around a-lot and he made sure we didn't want for anything and it really drove me closer to him.

However, I carried another burden around, and I was devastated. It was a sad situation and I went back to what I knew. I end up having my daughter and kept the secret from her that I didn't know who her father was for eleven years. I took her around his family like she was apart, his mother accepts her but he didn't.

The guy who I didn't want to be her father, was her father all along. I went through not knowing who my second child's father was, but that didn't stop me from sleeping around. This was the darkest time in my life I just did what was comfortable.

My son father best friend continued to come around he was taking us back and forth to places, and making sure we didn't need anything we were just friends. He helped me out a lot with my kids. He also had met some of the guys I was sleeping around with because he was always around. This man kept coming around helping me, everywhere we went he was there to pick us up. By him coming around so much we started catching feelings for each other and eventually it happened, I felt so bad and cried myself to sleep that night. Yes, I felt bad when it first happened, but I didn't stop it from happening. We continued to have sex, and we both knew it was wrong. I was still sleeping around with the other guys I didn't care, I was looking for love and I thought the guys will love me. I was having different guys over. I was telling the kids that they were relatives. Some days I would get a babysitter and go where they were. I was all over the place, I was a hot mess. I was definitely not being a good example for my children I was too busy chasing guys. I thought they had money and they were going to take care of me and my kids. I didn't even see how it was affecting my children. All I was worried about was pleasing my flesh and looking for love in all the wrong places. I was doing this all in my twenty and thirties in the club, after hours, trying seeing who I could meet next. I was looking for love when the kids were at grandma's house on weekend, I was out there.

The attention I was getting made me feel so beautiful and wanted. There were rumors that I had HIV and other diseases, which wasn't true but I wasn't exempt from it. The way I was going on with my life it was nothing but Grace God who saved me from that. I made the decision to sleep around.

During all this, I got pregnant for the third time, and her father was my son father best friend. He didn't claim her because of my pattern. I tried to convince him that she was his. He didn't claim her until someone in his family said that she looked like him. At this time this was the man I was trying to be serious

41

with, I knew it was wrong because he was my son father best friend, but he gave me attention, he made me feel wanted, it was hard for me to be faithful. However, our relationship was not healthy it went from loving each other to abusing each other this went on for some time. We were cheating on each other, fighting in front of the children. There was plenty time he told me he didn't want me but I was so messed up in the head I was forcing him to be with me. Everywhere he went I was there, acting a fool with other girls he was sleeping with. It was bad I didn't know who I was at this time. I was still sleeping around, going back and forth, to him and the other guys. My kids were seeing all this.   Eventually, I ended up getting pregnant with my fourth child and got an abortion, my third child was still in diapers and I just didn't want it.

Two years later I get pregnant again by this same man that was abusing me physically and emotionally. We moved to Jefferson, City Missouri together to start our lives. I wanted to get away and start fresh. In Jefferson City, I with still dealing with abuse, things did not change. After I had my son I still stayed with him. A year later I let him go and end up moving back to Kansas City.

Chapter 5:

Got Away With It

I started shoplifting and writing bad checks. I was experiencing things that I saw some of my friends doing. Shoplifting began with a job I had I saw everybody else stealing and getting away with it, so I started stealing. It became an every weekend thing, seeing my kids with decent clothes on every day made me feel like I was the best mother. I used to dress my kids up every day showing them off. I felt like I was really taking care of my kids. It had gotten so bad that I was taking them to the store with me, using them as a shield. I was planting seeds, whether they were good or bad, I was planting them. I was addicted to what I was doing and I could not stop. I was getting away with it so I kept doing it. It got to the point where I was stealing anything, I was a follower, and everything I saw someone else do I would try to do it. I didn't care at all; I was only worried about pleasing my flesh and dressing my kids, and I wasn't teaching them anything. I had a "who's next?" attitude; and I did just what I wanted. I got caught by the police a couple of times but as soon as I got out I was at it again. My kids had so many clothes, that they had trash bags full in their closets. It was like almost every day they were wearing something new.

My kids were growing up, they were getting so big and I had so much going on around them. I was thinking that I had been a good mother to them because they dress better than me when I was growing up. I kept the house clean and I made sure we always had food to eat.

It's more to it than dressing your kids. As I became older I had to understand that kids are not dolls, they need to be taught, loved and cared for.

Going through the struggles with my kids, I sat and wonder where they got some of their ways. I began to see a lot of me in them and the seeds that I was planting. Remember your children watch everything you do.

Chapter 6:

Not Listening

I was really disrespectful to my mother and other members of the family. I thought I was grown and could do and say what I wanted.

I had to experience some unnecessary things, but if I had just listened I could have saved myself from some heartache and pain. I thought, "This is fun, this is the way my life is".

I was showing my girls how to find love through different guys, and I sit and wondered where they got it from. Like the song says, "They get it from her momma." I was just doing what I felt was right. We only do what we're taught, whether it's right or wrong. My momma did it, so I thought it was okay. I'm not saying everything she taught me was wrong, but she only did what she knew. I don't blame her for any of my mistakes. I was not listening and I was being disrespectful to her and I knew it wasn't right. Oh God, how I had to repent and tell her I was sorry. You only get one mother and you are supposed to honor and respect her and a lot of times I didn't. I have learned from many of my mistakes. My mother and I are now best of friends and I wouldn't change that for the world.

The bible says in Deuteronomy 5: 16 Honor your father and mother as the Lord your God commanded you. Then you will live long, full of life in the land the Lord your God is giving you.

Chapter 7:

I heard His Voice

I remember telling my mother, that I'm tired of living my life like this. I was tired of waking up and doing the same thing every day. My mother said, "if you are tired, then change it." I told her I wanted to get my high school diploma and she said go get it. I heard about this test you can take online to get your high school diploma. I got the information, took the test and passed it. I immediately enrolled in cosmetology school. I always wanted to do hair, but I couldn't because I dropped out of school. I started cosmetology school and I was very excited. This was one of my dreams and it came true. I could not believe that this was real. This girl that messed up last night gets to go to cosmetology school. I was working at a home health care agency at this time helping the elderly, taking care of my mother, and going to hair school. Sixteen months later I graduated with my cosmetology license. I have finally accomplished something! All my life I thought I could not finish anything, but I did. My heart was so proud.

I knew I wanted to change my life and the only way I could was if I start going to church and that's what I did. I started to attend church, just to say I went. I wasn't paying attention to the Pastor, my mind was wandering around thinking about what I'm going to do when I get out here. I was saying one thing, but my actions were doing another. I got so comfortable with sleeping around, and drinking, clubbing it I didn't see a way out. I told my kids, we will go to church every other Sunday and that's what we did. (Who tell their kids that?) I was going to church for about a year, every other Sunday.

One Sunday morning, I was at church and I heard the Holy Spirit loud and clear saying I need you to take care of my people. I said to myself, "How am I going to take care of your people when I can't take care of myself?" I'm not worthy to take care of your people; I do all kinds of wrong. Who am I? I write bad checks, I shoplift and I'm sleeping around. I was trying to come up with every excuse not to do His will. I knew I wanted to change. I knew I wanted to get my life right but didn't know how. It was scary, what was I supposed to do.

God used my brokenness to help others, I was in shock! So, that is what I did, two months later, I started a program called Teen Watch, helping my family and their friends. I didn't know what I was going to do, but I did it. I was working with kids, to keep them off the streets. I came up with the plan, wrote it down, and spoke with some friends, some supported my idea and some didn't. I went to the church that I attended at that time and asked the pastor can I use this facility to have my group meetings and he said yes. Had my first meet and greet with my family and friends, and my pastor at that time told me everything that will go wrong. I didn't let what he said to stop me from doing what God told me to do. I decided not to use the church and I moved on. I teamed up with the Kansas City Public Library and asked the manager if I could use one of a room every Wednesday to meet with my new group. She said yes, but the only requirement was, if any other kids come into the library they must able to come into the program. I said sure they can come. I was so excited for my first youth program. I was still a mess, but I knew God was working on me.

I met up with the kids every Wednesday at 6:30, some I picked up and some had their own ride. Some of my friends came out to help me, and I was coming up with different ideas every week so they could walk away with something positive. I had speakers coming in and we did different activities. Teen Watch went on for a couple years and then I teamed up with another teen group, called Front Porch alliance; it was a nonprofit organization, I was excited about the endless possibilities. My kids had a blast, met a lot of other kids and spent quite some time with them. The teens were looking up to me they saw things in me that I didn't see in myself. In my mind I was thinking: What am I showing them? I can't tell them not to do certain things because when I leave them, I'm doing it. I just kept saying, "How am I going to change?" I kept doing the same thing; I just had more to tell them. God started changing me when I started giving.

God was showing me what He can do in my life

if I just let Him.

Chapter 8

Fatherless Son

Raising my first son alone without his father was something I didn't plan to do. We both had hopes and dreams to have a family and to get our lives together. I was devastated when he got killed; it was the darkest time in my life. I was excited to have my first child, I felt like I was grown and had it all together. I had someone who truly loved me that I didn't have to drop my pants for it.

As he got older I often wondered how can I explain to him that his dad was killed when I was seven months pregnant. It took me a while to tell him because I knew he wouldn't understand, so I waited until he got little older. I tried to be a great mother, knowing that boys need their fathers in their lives. His father friends were coming around talking to my son and telling what his father was liked.

As time went by he was getting older, he was doing okay in school, hanging out with his friends. It was told by one of my friends that my son had joined a gang. He was twelve-years old at that time. I didn't believe it, but all the signs were there. I just didn't want to face it. I was embarrassed and ashamed; I was shocked! I kept saying, "This is not true; he would not do anything like that." Years went by; I was trying to stop him from hanging out with certain people, but he would sneak and do it anyway. I reached out to family members to help me, but some of them were doing the same things as him. I tried to stay on him and keep him out of trouble, but he kept denying that he was in a gang. He would say, "Momma I'm not in a gang!!! I put him in sports, tried to keep him busy, and kept him close. You can't always see everything your child is doing

People in my family knew he was in a gang and never said anything. My son did not know his dad, but he had some of the same traits if not more as him. Things I was hearing about him were unbelievable; it was heart-breaking, and I couldn't do anything but cry. There were rumors in our area that someone wanted to kill him. He was in the gang really deep; he started to not come home. I was called the police and they would not help me. He was running away a lot, he would come back home and then he will do it again. There were days when I didn't know where my son was at all. I was really scared for him and didn't know what to do. What I heard about him was not the child I raised I was scared for my family. I was letting his friends come over just to keep him close and out of the streets.

He was caught in a stolen car, and I had to go pick him up from a detention center. I fussed and punished him, but that didn't work. He would just go outside and hang with the same boys and do the same things.

During middle school, they diagnosed him with a learning disability. When I told him about the learning disability he was ashamed. It seemed like he just gave up on school. If he didn't know how to do the school work, he would just act out in class. He became the class clown, and everyone loved him in school. He did not have to be in the streets; he just chose to be. Can you imagine how I was feeling?

As time went on; he was getting older and more into the streets. It was a sunny summer day and he was at my sister's house when I got a phone call saying my son was about to be killed. I got there as quickly as possible, to see my brother, my uncle, and their friends with guns. There were police and helicopters everywhere. I ran to my son and told him, I have to get you away from here, Today! He said, "Momma! I didn't do anything, they came after me." I said, "I told you not to hang out. Why are you looking for trouble? Why?" I said, "You have to go!" This was hard for me. I had to get him in a safe place, so the next day

I put him on the plane to his grandmother (his dad's mom in Atlanta). I sent him to go stay with her for a while, seeing my son pack and leave was heartbreaking; I couldn't do anything but cry. In my mind, I was thinking, "I have to get my son away from here." My son was thinking I didn't want him, but I was trying to save him. He made it to Atlanta the next day with his grandmother and was there about a year, going to school when he wanted to, and hanging out. He has found more boys he could hang out with, and they started their own gang. When you think you're getting him away from the trouble I had to realize that he was the trouble.

While he was gone, my house was broken into twice in one week; come to find out, it was his friends who did it the ones I used to let come over my house. I called and told my son what was going on, but he didn't believe it was his friends; he got upset and hung up. At that time, I said he don't have to come back; he should stay up there until he graduates.

His grandmother called me from time to time, saying he wasn't going to school; he was stealing from her and being disrespectful. She put him on the phone, and I tried to talk to him, but everything I said went in one ear and out the other. I felt like that I was a bad mother, he was upset with me, and I didn't know what to do. A year went by and his grandmother sent him back to me, but I wasn't ready for him. I was still living in the same place, and I had to wait a year to move because I was on section 8. I picked him up from the bus station, and I let him know he could not stay with me because there were still rumors, that other gang members were going to kick my door down and kill us if they couldn't get you. I was scared out of my mind and my other children were scared. We had to watch our back everywhere we went. I had some people watch my house I didn't let my kids go anywhere without me unless it's was with their grandmother. I called my mother and asked her if he could come live with her for a year in Jefferson City, Missouri. At that time, I was planning to move to Dallas, Texas. She agreed, and I took him there and enrolled him in school. I did everything I could to get him comfortable. He didn't want to be there; he felt like I did not want him. He felt the same way I felt as a foster child. I loved my son, and I was just trying to save his life. He would ask why everyone had a daddy and he didn't. I said, "Son, I can't tell you why you don't have a father, but I can try my best, to be a good mother." I would tell him that this move was just temporary. I would call my mother and the school and check on him, but he still wasn't doing right. He was getting into trouble down there too. He was never at my mother's house or at school. He was seventeen-years-old and one grade away from graduating; he was almost there. I kept telling him not to give up on school. "He was saying mama school is hard for me, I said son please don't so he give up." He did!

He got in the streets and no one could tell him anything. It was told to me that he started his own gang called Cutthroat, and he was a hot commodity in Jefferson, City. He was always in fights, shoot-outs and was holding people hostage, doing awful things to people.. What I was hearing about my son was unbelievable. All I could say was, "I didn't raise him like this. Where did I go wrong?" All the police in this little town in Jefferson, City Missouri knew my son's name. It was crazy; it was like a movie. My son was like the King Pin in Jefferson, City. There was so much going on; my move wasn't coming fast enough. I still had five months to go and I was going back to get my son and move.

I was trying to talk to my son and he wouldn't answer his phone for me, the only time I hear from him is when he was in trouble.

Finally, I was ready to move to Dallas Texas and I had to go back to Jefferson, City to get my son, but he didn't want to come because he had two girls pregnant. I was really upset about that, there I was leaving him again, he was now eighteen years. Moving to Dallas, Texas with three kids and leaving my son behind, was so hard but I did not have a choice. Not only that I'm leaving my son in Missouri, but I'm about to be a grandmother at the age of thirty-five. I was so ready to go and start a new chapter in my life with all four of my children, but I left with three. This move to Dallas, Texas was to save my son, and he didn't even come. He stayed in trouble and continued to do things out of the will of God. Then he made up another gang called Duffy, and it was big. Girls and boys were involved, and it hit the news. I could not stop him. I was not there; I was ten hours away, and all I could do was Pray and "ask God please don't take him, but sit him down." He went to jail for about six months and got out and did the same thing. It seems like every time I was leaving the church, I would get that phone call about my son, and what he was doing in the streets. I tried to talking and praying with him and letting him know he doesn't have to live that way. You can come to Dallas, Texas to change your life, he didn't listen. He was going back and forth to jail, getting out and doing the same thing. I was trying to help children and my son was in another state hurting people. He went back to jail again and this time they were going to give him some time because he violated his probation.

My son, he is twenty- three years old and been in and out of trouble since he was twelve. He didn't understand what he was going through and what I was going through. As I sat in that courtroom, on January 26, 2017, to hear all the things that the court was saying about my son and what he did, it made me want to give him some time. All I can do is cry, it is so sad to see my son go through this, but he chose that life for himself.

They wanted to offer him 70 months in jail; his lawyer offered 40 months, but the judge gave him 30 months. I really think if we had not come to court to support him, they would have given him more time. Can we say Grace!!! God is covering my son once again and I'm so thankful. The way my son was going on, I thought I was going bury my child, but God had something different for him. We went there thinking he was going to get 40 months in jail, and the prosecutor wanted to give him 70 months in jail but walked out with only 30 months in jail. I sat and watched how God was working in that courtroom, how the judge opens up to my son and encourage him about his life. He didn't have to do that, but he did.

But to each one of us, grace has been given as Christ appointed it.   Ephesians: 4:7

For it is by grace that you have been saved, through faith-this is not from yourself it is a gift of God-not by work so that no one can

boast Ephesians 2:8-9

Chapter 9:

My Angel

Raising my daughter, I thought I knew who her daddy was until she was three-years of age. Her father and I had taken a blood test and the results came back saying HE IS NOT THE FATHER! Wow! I was devastated and heartbroken. I thought I knew who her father was. I said to myself there was no way that this could be true, but it was. The man who I thought was her father was incarcerated and he had doubts. He was not the father but she had already been named after him. There was nothing I could do about that. His mother stated that she will always be her grandchild no matter what. Years went by and there was a guy that kept coming around saying that she was his baby.

This guy was in college and he was trying to get it together. The other guy was in still in jail. I was being young and dumb I didn't want that life for her instead, I wanted a street man. I continued to avoid him and got another guy tested and again the results were YOU ARE NOT THE FATHER. Here I am with two kids one whose father was deceased and the other I did not know who her father was. Heartbroken trying to raise them the best way I knew how. As my daughter grew up, she became very active in school. She was very involved and was just as sweet as she could be. Her teachers liked her a lot. I never seemed to get any bad reports and her grades were always good. I noticed she was starting to like boys and I did not like that. I was still bringing different guys around her and I wondered where she got it from. I was so blind and I did not know what I was doing would have a big effect on her life, but it did. With all that going on I was still sleeping around with different guys.

I just went on with my life, doing whatever I wanted to do. I felt as if as long as my kids were taken care of I could do what I wanted. I didn't care; I was looking for love.

When my daughter turned fourteen-years-old, she asked me, "Momma! Momma! Why I don't know who my daddy is?" I said, "You will soon," but she kept asking me. Finally, I went and had the paternity test done with the guy that was coming around saying that he was her father. Two weeks later: YOU ARE THE FATHER! In my mind, I felt like a child should not have to suffer because her momma does not know how to keep her legs closed. She cried, I cried, I felt so much weight just lifted off my shoulders. I was so happy and she was too. I knew who my daughter's daddy was, finally the shame and guilt left. I tried to build a relationship with her real father I got in touch with him and he already knew about the test because he had gotten the results at the same time I did. He was upset when we talked and I could not say anything but I'm sorry. I assumed that I was saying I'm sorry helped and he was going to be in her life, but he wasn't. Two years later we moved away. He was paying child support, but somehow he managed to stop doing that.

She was in high school, about to graduate with honors. I saw a lot of myself in her when dealing with the boys. I didn't want her to be like me and experience some of the things that I did. I was very strict with her and she got sneaky. I thought she was staying after school all those time like she told me but, most of the time she was leaving school with a boy. She graduated from high school with honors and had a graduation dinner with family and friends. We had a nice time, everyone was giving speeches, telling her how proud they were of her, and she was just crying. My auntie said, "Niece, that's not a happy cry something else is going on with her." Days went by, my daughter and I had a misunderstanding, and she left and ended up in Kansas, City. Her uncle picked her up from Dallas, Texas without my permission. I was really mad at the uncle for pulling that move and not contacting me to see what was actually going on.

Weeks went by and I get a text from my daughter saying that she has something to tell me. I said, "What?" The next text came in, "Momma, I am pregnant!" At that time, I was at my salon talking to a friend, and I just threw the phone when I read that and said, "WHAT THE HELL!" It's was an awful feeling when you realize the daughter you thought could do no wrong was doing wrong all the time. She was telling me she was at school and running off with a boy. I really believed her because she had good grades, she was on her way to graduating and she was actually a good child. I was heartbroken, upset, mad, and angry. All this time, she had been lying to me saying that she hadn't had sex and she really was. I said the first thing that came to my mind, "I am done with you!' Let your uncle care for you, you cannot come back here." I said some stuff to her that I never thought I would say, but I did. I felt so empty, I couldn't stop crying. I was taking it out on the other two kids, getting on them like they were the ones who sent me the text. I was going to church upset, really not paying attention to the word. My Pastor had to help me see it another way. I couldn't see it any other way until he explained it to me. All I wanted to do is beat her up. I was so angry I literally wanted to physically fight my daughter. I knew that wasn't going to help, but that's how I felt at the time. This was like a nightmare.

She came home on the Greyhound, and she was showing I couldn't punch her like I wanted to but I let her have it. She was crying; I was crying. The gift from God is here and I couldn't do anything but accept that I was going to have another grandchild. She always said she wanted to go to college and she did with her baby. She attended Texas Woman's University and majored in education. It just showed me that she didn't let anything stop her. She was going to make something out of herself and she was on it. I'm proud to say she did more than I ever did at that age and I know it can happen if you just put your mind to it and go for it. I got plenty of phone calls and texts from her, talking about how hard it is, how some days are easier than others. She had to find a babysitter for her son and make things happen. God steps in all the time, and she recognizes it.

Philippians 4:13 (I can do all thing through Christ that strengthens me) and used it.

Regardless if you have a child or not you can still go to school, go after your vision and dreams. You have more than just yourself to make proud.

Chapter 10:

She's Mines

I had my third child, by a man that I was with, but he did not acknowledge her as his child. When I had my daughter, I was alone once again in the hospital, feeling like I am going down the same rode like the last two. I was supposed to be in a relationship, but I was all alone. When I got out the hospital I went home to that same man, that didn't claim my daughter. I didn't know my worth, my mind was saying one thing but actions were doing another. I didn't want to be by myself, I came to realize that I was already by myself. He didn't start claiming her until somebody in his family said she looked like him.

Time went on, my daughter started daycare she was really doing great. Her father was doing what he could when he wanted to do. She was cute and as sweet as could be. I was thinking that it didn't affect her but it did. She was very bright in school but sneaky. She was getting good grades, she was also involved in African dance and that what she was doing until we moved to Dallas, Texas.

She was twelve-years of age when I moved to Dallas, Texas. I got her enrolled in school, she did great, no real issues but a bad attitude. As she got older, she started high school and she started hanging around the wrong folks. She started experiencing things that were not right. I moved out of Seagoville, Texas to an area called Pleasant Grove, it was told to me that Pleasant Grove was the a bad neighborhood. I didn't know that until I moved there. That's when things really began to change with her. She began to run away and doing things she wasn't supposed to do. Some days she skipped school, and some days she didn't go at all, this was not like her. I was shocked, but I knew it had a lot to do with the environment we were in because all the other kids were doing wrong things. I just knew she wanted to fit in and she didn't have to.

I wanted so much more for her, I asked her older sister if she can come and stay with her in Denton Texas. I told her "she has to get out of this neighborhood". Her older sister took her in and she was excited because they have always been close. I can tell that this was a great move for her. She was going to school every day, she had a job and was even helping her older sister with her baby. They got along well and were always encouraging each other.

My oldest daughter was a big help throughout that time. In 2017 my daughter graduated from Denton high school, I was beyond proud because there was a time, a couple years ago where she was skipping school days at a time. Now she is in college at UNT Dallas as a freshman studying child development. I am very proud of her. God is truly amazing.

Chapter 11

Watch for the Signs

Carrying my last son for nine months I didn't know that he will grow up with mental issues. I didn't have any issue with his birth, but when he turned three-years of age that's when the behavior issues begin.

I told myself that I will raise him different from my previous son. I thought I knew a little bit more. All I knew is that I did not want my son to be in the streets. He was three years of age when the behavior started in daycare. When I picked him up from daycare it was always something, he was constantly hitting or fighting someone. He even tried to kill the animals at the daycare, it was embarrassing. I was thinking he was just a child, and that's what kids do. Many days he will be playing out front and literally trying to hurt himself, jumping off the porch, hitting his head and all I can say "He's all boy," I was ignoring the signs. As time went by, daycare days were coming to an end, and it was now time for school. I knew that the daycare provider was ready for him to go, she had to have plenty of patients to deal with him daily. I was excited, that all four of my children are in school, daycare days are over.

In early childhood I was very involved, I was at the school daily getting to know the teachers, volunteering in the classroom, going on field trips. When I wasn't at the school my phone was ringing, the teacher was calling me about my son behavior, when I was there he didn't act like that. There were days that I couldn't stop what I was doing to go up there, so I sent my cousin who works in that field at the time to go see what was going on. She reported back to me stating that my son was acting out, hitting and fighting with other students. This went on for the whole early childhood experience, I was getting phone calls every day telling me to come pick him up, teachers were saying he has to go for today.

This was not just one time it started happening

often. I was really getting frustrated, saying to

myself why are these teachers picking on my

son, he was only three-years-old and what can

a three-year-old be doing in this classroom that

was causing so much commotion. I spanked his

butt daily, and that didn't work. I didn't see

these issues in our home he was my last child,

my baby boy. If I was to keep leaving my job

early to go see about my son, I would

eventually I lose my job. It was so sad and

embarrassing, trying to figure out what to do.

He's five-years-old now headed to

kindergarten, on to another school. He had the

same behavior issues but bigger, when we were at home, he was a normal kid, no outburst, no behavior issue or anything. I was telling his dad to help me, he didn't know how to, I began to deal with his behavior alone.

Every year, I was at the school having meetings with the teachers and the staff about my son's behavior, and they agreed that he needed to be tested. I said tested for what and what type of test. They were saying he has some behavior issue and we need to test him for ADHD (attention-deficit hyperactivity disorder). I decide to let the school test him, his daddy said no. I said my son needs some help! The school tested him and they diagnosed my son with ADHD. (If your kid needs help get them some help.) They gave me resources for a doctor and counselor that can assist me throughout this process. His father was very upset about the situation and he didn't do anything to make it better. On the other hand, I had to do what was best for my son. Seeing the doctor and counselors, really gave me hope. The doctor was saying things like, if I do what they ask me to do then my son is going to be ok, which was taking medicine and seeing the counselor once a week. I started it but I wasn't consistent. I had so many people in my ear telling me what to do and what not to do with my son.

As far back as I can remember, he had a smile and laughter, as he got older, the smile was fading away. He wasn't on the meds consistently; I was just going on with my daily routine. Not only that, he had behavior issues and couldn't focus in school at all, he was behind. I was trying to figure out what was wrong with my son. They told me and I didn't take it seriously, he was always in trouble. His grades failing and teachers were calling me daily. I felt like I worked there - that's how much I was at school. Everyone knew I was his mother when he was about seven-years-old we went back to the doctor and counselors, trying to get him help again. The doctor said to me, "You have to be willing to get him the help he needs. Don't wait until the trouble happens and then seek the help. You have the resources, just use them." Unfortunately, all they did was prescribe him different meds. I had been giving him the medication daily, and I told the doctors, "This cannot be it, it is not working!" I did not know that he wasn't swallowing the medicine until my daughter told me years later. As years went by his behavior continued, I was spanking him and punishing him, and that didn't work.

At this time I was preparing to move to Dallas, Texas looking forward to this new start for him. We moved to a little town called Seagoville Texas, I enrolled him in the elementary school, I immediately spoke to the staffs and explain to them about his history, I didn't want his behavior to be a surprise. Two weeks into school the issue begins, he wasn't on any medicine, I was really in denial that something was really wrong with my boy. He was getting suspended from school and kicked off the bus. I was feeling that teacher didn't like my son, so I would go to the school with this wall up, ready to attack anyone one who says anything negative about my child. He is my son, my baby, my last child what is going

on. Every school I put him there were

behavior issues. We had to move out of

Seagoville into a place where I could afford,

which was Pleasant Grove and it wasn't a great

neighborhood, I didn't realize that before I

move there. I enrolled him in middle school, let

him go outside and play with the other kids, his

behavior really was outrageous.   He started

hanging with the wrong crowd, getting into a

lot of trouble. I was at school meetings at least

twice a week, and he was getting suspended

and kicked off the bus on a regular.

My son started running away, being disrespectful to me and anyone he came in contact with. This situation wasn't getting any better. No doctor, no medicine, can help my son this situation was bigger than me. He was full of anger and I didn't know where it came from. If I said no or anything he didn't like he would get up my face. My son and I were bumping heads daily, I didn't like the way he was talking to me, and the way he was acting in school or at church. I attack every situation and didn't give him any solution about his behavior.

He started bucking me and he would get up in my face. I felt like he was really trying to hurt me. This behavior made me really dislike my kid and it got to the point where he wanted to fight back. He was thirteen-years-old and I was thinking "Oh my God, my child is fighting me. What is a mother supposed to do?" He was really fighting me back, and I wanted to kill him. The police came and took him out of the house and called me to come pick him up. I felt like, "This is crazy! Is this really happening in my house? The kid I raised from birth is really disrespecting me." As he got older, the problem got bigger and bigger, and the boy got stronger and stronger. I had to realize that my son needed help, regardless of what people had to say, I had to do what's best for him, He was angry; I was angry. However, him and I going back and forth did not work. Police and CPS got involved and made matters worse. This went on for some years. It got to the point where he started lying, stealing, and even running away for weeks. I cried, screamed, and prayed but he still was acting out. I kept saying, "God is going to change this mess into a message." Some days I feared for my life. I didn't know what he was going to do; when he was angry, he turned into someone totally different. Many days I locked my bedroom door and slept with one eye open.

Can you imagine a mother fearing for her life? It got to the point that I had to go get some mace and a stun gun for protection from my son. I was tired of him getting up in my face every time he got angry and the thing didn't go his way. Everybody was in my ear saying, "Don't give up on him." Believe me, there were plenty of days that I wanted to. I had been riding this roller coaster for a while, and I was fighting my son, but he was not the real enemy. I felt like I had to attack every situation when he disrespected me. My first mind was to knock him down every time he did that. It was really hard for me; I was hurting myself daily. He was constantly running away for days at a time and just doing what he wanted to do. When you get tired, you get tired, and I couldn't change him, but I could change myself. I was calling around seeking help and didn't get the help that was needed. I continued to call the police station in order for someone to take what I was telling them seriously. It got physical to the point where my own son tried to hit me. My husband ended up getting involved to protect me.

Going through this caused a wedge in our family and relationship. My girls felt as if their mother was being mistreated, so most of the time they didn't want to deal with him. As of today, we are still going through, he is fifteen-years-old and is locked up because he continued to run away. As I go see him weekly for the therapy session, some weeks are better than others. I notice that he still have a lot of anger and this will not be an overnight process. This is going to take a lot of work and a lot of prayer and patience.

As I learn that every action doesn't need a reaction. I have to learn how to deal with a kid who has a mental health issue.

When it comes to your kids and you have all the signs - doctor notes, teachers behavior reports saying your child needs help - please don't ignore it. Get your baby some help so he or she can function in society. This situation has been hard for me; there have been many days I wanted to put him out and not let him come back. I know he is full of anger, but I'm not the one he is angry with.

As I grow in Christ, I'm learning I have to change some of my actions to avoid conflict. Families are supposed to love one another. Believe me when I say kids need role models, mentors, and someone consistent in their lives, It makes a big difference.

If your mind is not right, none of the things you do will matter. Get your baby some help! He is fifteen-years-old now and not in my home and some days are better than others, and I pray that things will get better.

What I have learned in the journey is that life is not easy. Continue to pray, and be specific in your prayers. Give it to God because God will fight your battle. Yes, this has been a learning experience, and I know God is not done. As I sit and think of where I came from and what I have overcome, I know we are going to make it through this. My son is going to grow up to be the man that God has called him to be.

Ephesians 6:12 says, "For we wrestle not against flesh and blood, but against principalities, against power, against the ruler of the darkness of this world, against spiritual wickedness in High places.

Chapter 12

Turning Around For Me

Moving from Kansas, City to Dallas, Texas was a big step for me and my family. My kids were sad and emotional about our move they did not want to move away from all their friends. I didn't know what I was going to do; I was ready to make a change in my life. My way out from Kansas City, was for me to make the decision to move, and I did. In July of 2011, I moved myself and three of my children out of Kansas City, I drove the biggest U-Haul and had my little Ford Taurus on the back of the trailer, I took everything with me. I wasn't planning on leaving anything behind, but my oldest son decided that he didn't want to come. I felt nervous and scared, about the big move, I knew it was time for me to go. I had never driven the biggest U-Haul before, by the time I made it to Oklahoma, we were halfway to my new start. We made it eighteen hours later and moved into a very nice home in Seagoville, Texas. Some of my former friends that I knew from Kansas City were already living in Dallas, and they came to help me unpack. They were very supportive throughout this transition. A day later the central air unit went out. Now imagine living in Dallas,Texas in the middle of July with no air conditioning. I was so frustrated, I did not know what to do, my landlord decided to put us in a hotel for about a week. I felt better and at ease about the situation. I could have gotten distracted, and went back home because of one downfall, however I had it in my mind that I am not going back and I still remain here Dallas, Texas six years later. I was not letting anything or anybody stop me from moving forward. I enrolled my kids in a school nearby the neighborhood. They were still sad about the move I knew as a parent I was making the best decision for them. I got a job in a Town East Mall at a hair salon called, (Mia Max Hair

Salon). I did enjoy working there, I just knew I wanted more and this was not it.

I moved from Kansas, City Missouri to Dallas, Texas with all my baggage everything that I thought I was leaving behind I brought it all with me. Although it was a fresh start I felt that I could not let go of my past.

I started doing the same things I did back home, looking for love, partying, and drinking. I also was going back and forth to Kansas City sleeping with a married man. For some odd reason going back to him made me feel wanted and loved. I knew it was wrong and something was really off about it, I felt convicted every time. This went on for about another year until one day, I was coming home from school and the Holy Spirit spoke to me, and said, "You are doing the same things you did in Kansas City. I thought you moved to change." I told myself: I've got to change; I'm in another state and no one knows me here. I told my friend that I was around that I was done drinking and I'm going to get my life together. I just knew it was time to stop playing with God. I knew that God would deliver me one day at a time and not all at once. I prayed to God to help me stop drinking and cussing and it happened. God was showing me what He can do, thank you God for deliverance. I told myself, I was going to go find a church home and get involved in church. One of the friends invited me to Another Chance Fellowship Church, where I still remain - the name just changed, not the word. I came into church with a lot of baggage, a lot of worries, shame, and guilt. As I listened to the pastor, he gave me the hunger to try God for myself. I started reading self-help books, taking notes in church and still walking out of church struggling. The battle is real! The flesh is weak! I was going on dates, trying to find someone to love me. I was still missing something. Have you ever been around a lot of people and still felt lonely? That was me, I felt so lonely growing up, and it started changing little by little when I started seeking God.

I enrolled at East Field College studying Social Work. I was trying to find something else to focus on so I didn't have to face my past. Not realizing that in order to go forward in life I had to face my past and deal with it to be set free. The only person I needed was Jesus, but I still wasn't quite there.

I got more involved in church; I was going Sunday, Wednesday, and Thursday every week. I was learning things I had never heard before, the pastor was teaching me. My life was changing little by little, I never thought

I could change. When I stopped drinking and cussing I knew then it was more and I wanted it.

I knew I wanted to work with kids, and I started a youth group called Teen Watch in Dallas. They learned how to give back, different life skills, how to work with others, and just being a better person. I had the whole block of kids in Seagoville, Texas at my house every Wednesday evening at 6:30. I was encouraging them, building a relationship with them, and just being there. This was the time I really began to tell my story and open up about some things that I have done. I really enjoyed those kids and I knew I still had some changing to do because now I had thirty-four- years old kids looking up to me. Not only did I see them on Wednesdays, I saw those kids daily. They would bring their report cards by the house, to show me. "Miss Carmen! Miss Carmen, look at what I did!" They would even tell me about their day. I felt important, and they were important to me.

We began to do a lot of volunteer work and giving back in the city of Dallas. We started feeding the homeless once a month, we also adopted a block called Teen Watch, that's when we had to clean the block up quarterly.

We did fundraisers and went on field trips, we had a great time. Our first experience going down under the bridge to feed the homeless was very emotional, the kids and I were crying, the ride back home was very quiet. We knew people were homeless but to see it and witness it, was very hard for us. However, they had to understand that this is reality. It is possible that we can all be down there living under a bridge.

Seeing people in the line waiting for food it just reminded me that my family and I were once there. I asked the youth- if they would like to keep doing it, and they said yes, and we did. God continued to give me different ideas to help others. Some I started, but some I didn't finish and some I still do today. For example, I started an organization called Flip Flop Drive, it consisted of collecting flip-flops and giving them out to kids that are in need. This event is always in June we would give away food, snow cones and popcorn. We also would paint the little girls' nails and teach young men how to tie a tie

I am so grateful to be able to give back, and we also have an event every school year called "Styles 4 Smiles Back to School Bash" were we give away free school supplies and also do hair. I started this in Kansas City and brought it to Dallas, Texas. By giving back I found the good in me and now that is my passion.

Styles 4 Smiles name came about when a friend of mines brought it to my attention, the saying was if you give me a smile and I will give you a style'. Which is how I got my own business started entitled Styles 4 Smiles. Not only do I love giving back but I also love doing hair and doing anything I can do to help others out.

In 2013, I was informed by the college I attended that I could no longer go there anymore due to not having a high school diploma. I did not realize that the test I took to get my High School Diploma back in 2006 wasn't legit. I used that same high school diploma to get into cosmetology school, and I graduated and got my license to do hair. I didn't get upset with the people but when I walked out of school, I wanted to scream and cry because my feelings were so hurt. I had been in college for two years ready to transfer to a university and I couldn't. I had to enroll in a GED program. I felt like I was starting all over again. I did enroll in a GED (General Education Diploma) program at a facility called Lift- Literacy Instruction of Texas and i remained there until I got my High School

Diploma. I was studying to GED however, GED program was really hard for me. As time went by another staff member told me about a new test called Hiset Exam. She also stated that some students were going back and forth to Oklahoma to take the test because it was not offered in Dallas at the time. I knew I had to commute back and forth to Oklahoma. I started to study for Hiset Exam in April 2016 and was a high school graduate by July 2016. I drove to Oklahoma five times and it was worth it. In between the course of my studies, I was having major issues with my youngest son.

I stayed focused on getting my high school diploma and I also got married in 2015. I never thought this would happen; I felt like I wasn't marriage material because of my past. It was so much going on at the time but I was determined not to give up and keep going. WON'T GOD DO IT! I have been here in Dallas for six years and it has been great. It's been a lot of ups and downs, but going through this was worth it. I never thought I would become the woman I am today. I am so grateful, if God can do this, then it's more.

I am a salon owner, high school graduate, college student, and wife and I'm still climbing that mountain. I haven't reached my purpose yet.

As I look back over my life, I see how I was stuck, I felt like there was no way out. I got comfortable and didn't want to take a step to move forward in my life. I didn't know that fear had a way of controlling me. I wanted more but was scared of failing. I didn't take a chance, not knowing I had already failed - failed myself. When I wanted it and God gave it to me, like my pastor says, "You can have as much as God as you want."

Chapter 13

But God

Getting to know God as my Father, my Creator is the best thing that ever happened to me. I thought that I would be perfect by now but that is not how God works. I will never be perfect but I can be better. As I walk this life of Christ that was a choice I made, I was tired of letting the devil use me as his slave. When you are so used to doing things that feel good and everyone around you is doing it, it is hard to let it go.

Having a relationship with God it has taught me that it is a daily walk. It is about spending time with him and getting to know Him, just like you would if you were dating someone. I have learned that my past is my past, and the reason why I have been through so much was so I can be able to talk about it and help someone and not hide behind it. If I didn't have a purpose in my life, I would have been dead and gone by now. Thank you God for saving me from myself, after all the mistakes I made He still used me and I am thankful and truly humble. I thank God for the people he placed in my life to help me grow and become the woman I am today.

Remember you can't make it in this world without God.

2 Corinthians 5:17 Therefore if any man be in Christ, he is a new creature: old thing have passed away; behold all things have become new.

Carmen Edwards Garnett

Made in the USA
Columbia, SC
09 March 2018